The Stability of Trees in the Winds of Grief

poems by

Phyllis Carito

Finishing Line Press
Georgetown, Kentucky

The Stability of Trees in the Winds of Grief

Copyright © 2019 by Phyllis Carito
ISBN 978-1-64662-061-6 First Edition
All rights reserved under International and Pan-American Copyright Conventions. No part of this book may be reproduced in any manner whatsoever without written permission from the publisher, except in the case of brief quotations embodied in critical articles and reviews.

ACKNOWLEDGMENTS

Previously published:
"Trees"—*barely a whisper* 2010
"Methuselah"—*Passager* Journal Winter 2019
"Tumbling" *Passager* Journal Fall 2019

Thank you to family and friends who always support me in my writing.

Poetry is my solace and my exploration. Writing poems for me is a process that can move from a phrase running through my head, ruminating about some small idea, to the poem slowly developing into shape.

I am ever grateful to my first readers, Regina, Pat, and Marcia for their insight and patience with my endless search for the correct words. Thanks to John Hoppenthaler and Sandra Longley, amazing poets, for reading and commenting on the work. Thanks to all who support my quest through poetry for the expression of emotion in the remembering of Roland.

Publisher: Leah Maines
Editor: Christen Kincaid
Cover Art: "Mother and Child" bronze public art in Villa Comunale Park,
    Sorrento Italy; photo by Phyllis Carito
Author Photo: Patricia Fecher, photographer
Cover Design: Elizabeth Maines McCleavy

Printed in the USA on acid-free paper.
Order online: www.finishinglinepress.com
    also available on amazon.com

Author inquiries and mail orders:
Finishing Line Press
P. O. Box 1626
Georgetown, Kentucky 40324
U. S. A.

Table of Contents

Preface xi

In the Next Life 1

Life's Punches 2

April 15, 2017 3

Topsy-turvy 4

Mother's Day 5

A Spec in the Universe 6

Among Strangers 7

Trees 8

Barking Up the Wrong Tree 9

Because life doesn't work that way 10

Tumbling 11

Ghost in the Photographs 12

Trees II 13

Waiting 15

A Year of Grief 16

Empty Rooms 17

What's next? 18

My eyes 19

Bittersweet 20

Methuselah 21

*For all the lives
enhanced by Roland's love and
especially for his children,
Raymond, and Vera Jean*

Preface

What holds us together when grief rips through us furiously gnawing at our insides, and spinning our heads like a tree tossed in a storm? For some it is faith, for some memories and time. For me it was the trees that kept rooted, that kept reminding me of life in the middle of the death. I would read my poems about trees, I read them to my son, Roland, in his last days, the quiet in the room, my voice, his shallow breathing until I heard myself say to let go like the leaves in Autumn, just let go. Somehow, the trees seemed the only stability as all our lives were being torn to shreds. What could I learn from the trees? They lost their leaves every year and stood through the ice of winter and then somehow those tiny buds would unfold again and I'd look up at a full tree, with leaves and birds; trees reaching to the immensity of sky. This was my comfort, my haven of trees.

Like the trees, I go through the seasons, my seasons of grief. I have a birch tree planted in my son's honor, I have days my anger blinds me, days my sorrow drains me, days I smile with a memory of his living that envelops me and brings some comfort.

This collection is in honor of my son, Roland Carito (1975-2017)

In the Next Life
> *How high does the sycamore grow—*
> *if you cut it down, you'll never know.*
> *—Pocahontas*

In the next life
I will be a tree
a stately redwood
reaching into the sky
catching the sea breeze off the Pacific
circled in family
grounded in fragrant moist soil.

Why a tree you ask?
Because they have roots
and they sway.

Life's Punches

The smart undercut
vibrates teeth, rings ears.
The quick jab to the temple
rattles the brain.

Weren't you just driving
down the street with music blaring?
Weren't you just picking apples with your family?

The unexpected blow—below the belt
with no referee for the call—it's just life.
Can you pick up your head—shake it clear?
Can your rubber legs get you to your knees, your feet?

Weren't you just working a career of giving?
Weren't you just playing and laughing
with your children?

Life stings, brings tears,
Challenges, fears, with pain and doubt.
Counts you down—how many rounds?
And too soon counts you out.

April 15, 2017
> *Love knows not its own depth until the hour of separation.*
> —Kahil Gibran

And just hold on

first to his fragile body
and then to every memory

And just hold on

because if you let go
the tears will flow

like a torrent that will never
ever stop

And just hold on

because there are children
and one day after another

And just hold on

even though nothing will mend
the hole in your heart

Topsy-turvy

It is about the youth now
and the best you can be
is a fading flower

It is about the youth now
until the world turns topsy-
turvy and the youth dies

You are still a fading flower
only now no one lifts
your head with joy

Mother's Day

When I arrived at the ocean
the rain and wind pounding
waves crashing out my anger
ripping at the sand tumultuously

Today's ocean ripples with lace edges
hugging the shore in cris-cross motion
washing smooth the sand;
a yellow ladybug without spots lands on me

Everything I knew wears a different lens;
but the ocean won't tell me why
his life was swept away
it just keeps repeating its swish in and tug out

There is a flood in me
seeping slowly under my doors
settling in low spots, hanging in the corners
washing away, washing away

A Spec in the Universe

At ocean side
feel the massive depth,
below holds more life
then you'll ever know

Pouring tears like salty seas
tried to keep them back
too deep for a breath to hold
to descend and ascend again

now with the rain I let them flow
wash away some of this pain
A whiff in the damp air carries a scent
of new life sprouting green.

Among Strangers

On the beach people gather
the mild waves direct their moods
the sun subdues them

I think of their lives and loves
I think of you coming back
as sea life—what would you be?

a dolphin—intelligent, happy, caring
a heron—great gentle bird
a pelican or a sea turtle?

Or, a person—a sweet little girl
How I hoped one day you would
tell the story to your daughter

of when she locked you out
of the Texas house, heat, and panic,
and breaking a window to get back to her

Some things just don't get to happen

Trees

"The lowest trees have tops"
—Sir Edward Dyer

Maybe I should go back to drawing them
Maybe I didn't see well enough how they were held
By root, spread by branch elbowing to limb, to twig.
What reach, what resting places—
If we can fly, crawl, climb to them.
I need to examine the crooks of trees
How they allow a change of direction.
Do the trees have more answers?
Shimmering in an ice glaze
Silhouetted against the night sky
Dressed up like ladies calling
Attention to themselves with bright feathers.

Did I take into account
DaVinci's understanding of their gnarls,
Frost's painting them "concerned with outer weather,"
and Muir's voicing how small we stood next to them.

Barking Up the Wrong Tree

again

of course you never learn

the first time
it's not deliberate

then you learn to live with
this mess you make of things

Because life doesn't work that way

there are spaces in my memory
mostly about getting from
there to here
I never remember all the time
it took
all the curves in the road
nauseous, head spinning;
I knew I would have this lonely
look-back time
but I thought it would be
twenty years from now.
so many times I've felt like
I've been free-falling
driving blind

I wanted to be a better mother
than mine
I wanted to be a married lady
for 50 years
my children secure
my grandchildren joyous
I wanted to embrace our life
I wanted to live the tradition
look back years later
holding all the good memories
pie-in-the-sky;

there are moments you take
for granted, moments you take
your eyes off the road

life leaves gouges
that blow out—
deflate the heart

Tumbling
> *"When the walls come tumblin' down..."*
> —J Mellencamp

jumbled like clothes in a washer
sometimes agitating against another piece
sometimes tangling
sometimes bashing against the sides

tossing from rim to bottom, side to side,
like a restless sleep in an endless night

snarled in grief to anger, anger to grief
some stains never wash out
some bleed across the fabric
some fade into the fibers leaving a shadow

continuous movement, entangled
shirt arms   pants leg   bra strap

tousled around and upside down
don't expect to forgive or accept
don't say it's god's will
don't say it will get buried deeper

still moments, so brief—water draining,
a deluge of tears—tumbling until every coin times out.

Ghost in the Photographs

You look out from all that is past.

All the ways you were showing us
your adventures from Florence to
Portland; you rode us along the coast
from sand dunes to rocky Devil's Elbow;
we drove up Pike's Peak, you and me—warm
to cold air as we rose, your confident
driving along the outside turns;
so many walks up Bash-Bish—your
home green, where talks were about
all the human foibles—that pained you;
all your concern for innocent children
so deep in your heart
so clear in your mind
so many places you tried to find
some relief;
your own children
brought out your joy—you held
them close, and touched them gently
with your wisdom.

All the places of your life become
before, and all the photographs
are the way we look back from after.

Trees II
    (After "Clouds" by Wislawa Szymborska)

To describe the trees
don't sit too close—
be distanced to view
scope, ground to sky
circle of shade

It is their nature
to hold onto
variations; and varying
bud to flower to leaf
to seed repeatedly

What kind of witness are they—
gathered in their branches
the homes of birds,
bugs, bushy tailed animals,
birth to death;
winged visitors perched
on the towering tiniest stem,
to view clear sky
for the next take off

Compared to trees
People are flighty
ungrounded

Next to trees
we the people
are unreliable
vain in spring and summer bodies
uncomfortable with winter nakedness

Let people lie, if they want,
under the canopy,
eat of their fruit and nuts

They are not bound
to perish...
even as we take their
sweet sap, withered limbs

But they can't run—
people saw them down
Or cause them disease
Or forget they live,
ever growing all their years—
giving breath to humans' vagabond life.

Waiting

for your daughter to call
for the electricity to come back on
                after the storm
the tomatoes to turn red on the vine
the broken bone to mend
for the roads to be cleared
                after the blizzard
for the weight of grief to lift
like your car idling at the red light
the fuel draining out of you

A Year of Grief

"Some things just happen and we don't get to know why."
(from Grey's Anatomy)

"First they die, and then they stay dead."
—Donald Hall

"I am living. I remember you."
—Marie Howe

It's coming on Christmas
they're cutting down trees
putting up reindeer...
I wish I had a river I could skate away on.
—Joni Mitchell

It's coming on a year
the twist of fate
that took him away
the shawl of grief
what's to be afraid of
he's already lost from our every day
memories and love stay
a year away—time
we gained and he'll never have
distance grows
distance grows

On the day I don't want
any one who knows
in my eyes of shadow
I want to sleep in a strange bed

It's coming on a year
of sorrow slowly
slipping away
slipping away

Empty Rooms

I pass a sign along Route 66
Guns and Honey for Sale
I don't stop to buy either—
everything I used to think is   gone from me.
Turn the heat up when I get home.
Grief turns me inward, but I keep moving,
propelled by blindness seeking light,
sun glistens on the last patches of snow
March trees' black masses turn to tipped gold buds
red tail hawk, puffed in winter fluff, eyes a next meal.
Turn the heat up when I get home.
Grief is love and memory,
pass a farmhouse with broken windows,
nested grey squirrel, under leaky roof, gnaws a next meal.
Once a family ate, slept, laughed and cried here;
forsaken home and hollowed heart—
everything I used to know is   gone from me.

What's next?

part woman, part tree, part lion.
I didn't know before
how we celebrate a woman,
pollute a tree, lose the jungle;

listen to the suffragettes
women libbers' echoes,
where is my ability
to confront the opposite sex?

know the pollutants are humans—
yet no lion leader roars in me,
I remain a follower
caged in my own limitations.

burrow myself in a grove of trees,
mean to protect the land;
breathe the air, sway with the wind
but can I share the bounty?

where to draw my power?
there is always a reminder
of weakness, and a fear,
unfounded and real as it might be.

persuaded that the terrible ending
is really a next beginning,
my pendulum always
leaves me swinging;

moving away from hurt
Can I find a steady footing?
embrace the tree and the lion,
save the woman again and again.

My eyes

my eyes are tired
even when I wake

sometimes so many tears fall
that they are squeezed dry

sometimes the brightness hurts
with all the unhappiness behind my eyes

I remember
my eyes used to smile

Bittersweet
    (June 6, 2018)

lingers
tear stung eyes
a wash of pain

lift our heads
to his memory
his bright eyes

pride and honor
for his humble
giving

and smile

Methuselah

I hear the grating chain saw
tearing into the sweet wood,
watch my neighbor
toppling tree after tree,
I weep for their years
scattered bark, crushed leaves,
centric slices oozing sap.

I read about Methuselah
kept hidden, protecting
4,874 years of bristlecone pine,
taking in all weather
reaching into the sky,
feathered and furred
safely at home in mighty branches.

I walk through my cherished grove
look up through the tree centers,
crossed branches, needles, cones,
applaud their growth,
steady myself on varied bark,
grateful to breathe in their pine,
whisper to them not to worry.

Phyllis Carito, MFA, Manhattanville College. She teaches Creative Writing at Columbia-Greene Community College. Her publications include a novel, *Worn Masks*, and a chapbook, *barely a whisper*. Other published work has appeared in *Stone Highway Review, Passager Journal, Inkwell Review, Voices in Italian Americana, Fired Up! (Berkshire Women's Writers) Oasis Journal, Vermont Literary Review,* and *Returning Woman Review*.

www.ingramcontent.com/pod-product-compliance
Lightning Source LLC
LaVergne TN
LVHW041520070426
835507LV00012B/1713